HAL•LEONARD
INSTRUMENTAL PLAY-ALONG

AUDIO ACCESS INCLUDED

PLAYBACK+
Speed • Pitch • Balance • Loop

ALTO SAX

To access audio visit:
www.halleonard.com/mylibrary

Enter Code
7266-7935-9435-0421

ISBN 978-1-4950-9055-4

Disney Characters and Artwork © 2017 Disney Enterprises, Inc.

Walt Disney Music Company
Wonderland Music Company, Inc.

DISTRIBUTED BY

HAL•LEONARD®
7777 W. BLUEMOUND RD. P.O. BOX 13819 MILWAUKEE, WI 53213

In Australia Contact:
Hal Leonard Australia Pty. Ltd.
4 Lentara Court
Cheltenham, Victoria, 3192 Australia
Email: ausadmin@halleonard.com.au

For all works contained herein:
Unauthorized copying, arranging, adapting, recording, Internet posting, public performance,
or other distribution of the printed or recorded music in this publication is an infringement of copyright.
Infringers are liable under the law.

Visit Hal Leonard Online at
www.halleonard.com

HOW FAR I'LL GO

ALTO SAX

Music and Lyrics by
LIN-MANUEL MIRANDA

© 2016 Walt Disney Music Company
All Rights Reserved. Used by Permission.

KNOW WHO YOU ARE

ALTO SAX

Music by OPETAIA FOA'I,
LIN-MANUEL MIRANDA and MARK MANCINA
Lyrics by OPETAIA FOA'I
and LIN-MANUEL MIRANDA

Moderately and freely

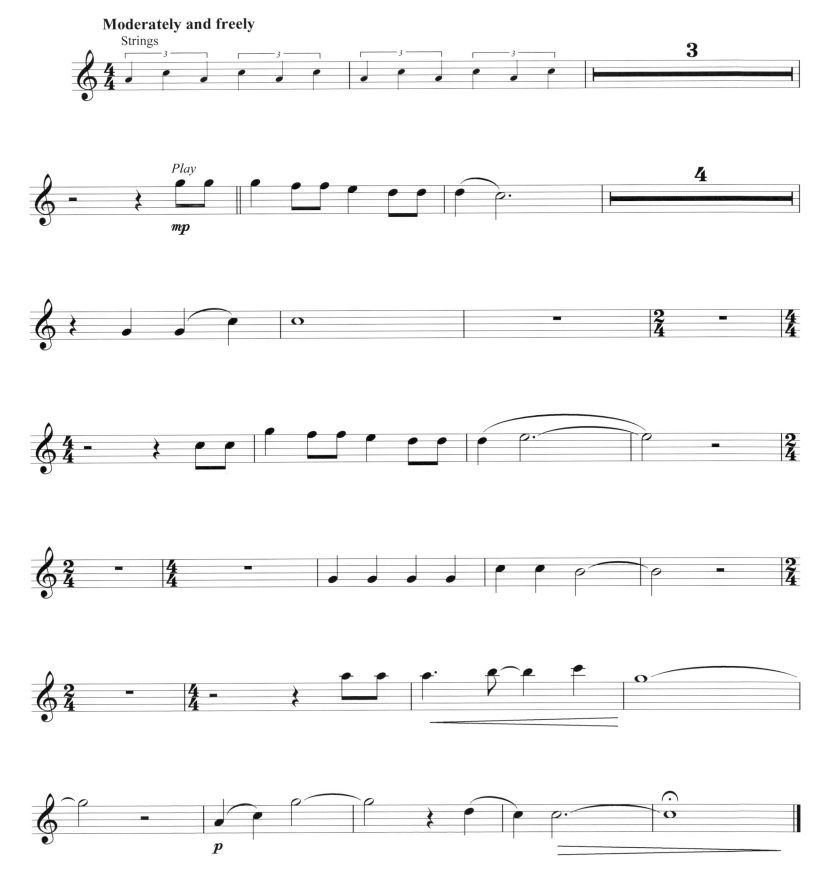

© 2016 Walt Disney Music Company and Wonderland Music Company, Inc.
All Rights Reserved. Used by Permission.

I AM MOANA
(Song of the Ancestors)

ALTO SAX

Music by LIN-MANUEL MIRANDA,
OPETAIA FOA'I and MARK MANCINA
Lyrics by LIN-MANUEL MIRANDA
and OPETAIA FOA'I

© 2016 Walt Disney Music Company and Wonderland Music Company, Inc.
All Rights Reserved. Used by Permission.

SHINY

ALTO SAX

Music by LIN-MANUEL MIRANDA
and MARK MANCINA
Lyrics by LIN-MANUEL MIRANDA

© 2016 Walt Disney Music Company and Wonderland Music Company, Inc.
All Rights Reserved. Used by Permission.

WE KNOW THE WAY

ALTO SAX

Music by OPETAIA FOA'I
Lyrics by OPETAIA FOA'I
and LIN-MANUEL MIRANDA

© 2016 Walt Disney Music Company
All Rights Reserved. Used by Permission.

WHERE YOU ARE

ALTO SAX

Music by LIN-MANUEL MIRANDA,
OPETAIA FOA'I and MARK MANCINA
Lyrics by LIN-MANUEL MIRANDA

© 2016 Walt Disney Music Company and Wonderland Music Company, Inc.
All Rights Reserved. Used by Permission.

YOU'RE WELCOME

ALTO SAX

Music and Lyrics by
LIN-MANUEL MIRANDA

© 2016 Walt Disney Music Company
All Rights Reserved. Used by Permission.

HAL•LEONARD INSTRUMENTAL PLAY-ALONG

Your favorite songs are arranged just for solo instrumentalists with this outstanding series. Each book includes great full-accompaniment play-along audio so you can sound just like a pro! Check out **www.halleonard.com** to see all the titles available.

12 Hot Singles

Broken (lovelytheband) • Havana (Camila Cabello) • Heaven (Kane Brown) • High Hopes (Panic! At the Disco) • The Middle (Zedd, Maren Morris & Grey) • Natural (Imagine Dragons) • No Place like You (Backstreet Boys) • Shallow (Lady Gaga & Bradley Cooper) • Sucker (Jonas Brothers) • Sunflower (Post Malone & Swae Lee) • thank u, next (Ariana Grande) • Youngblood (5 Seconds of Summer).

___ 00298576	Flute	$14.99
___ 00298577	Clarinet	$14.99
___ 00298578	Alto Sax	$14.99
___ 00298579	Tenor Sax	$14.99
___ 00298580	Trumpet	$14.99
___ 00298581	Horn	$14.99
___ 00298582	Trombone	$14.99
___ 00298583	Violin	$14.99
___ 00298584	Viola	$14.99
___ 00298585	Cello	$14.99

12 Pop Hits

Believer • Can't Stop the Feeling • Despacito • It Ain't Me • Look What You Made Me Do • Million Reasons • Perfect • Send My Love (To Your New Lover) • Shape of You • Slow Hands • Too Good at Goodbyes • What About Us.

___ 00261790	Flute	$12.99
___ 00261791	Clarinet	$12.99
___ 00261792	Alto Sax	$12.99
___ 00261793	Tenor Sax	$12.99
___ 00261794	Trumpet	$12.99
___ 00261795	Horn	$12.99
___ 00261796	Trombone	$12.99
___ 00261797	Violin	$12.99
___ 00261798	Viola	$12.99
___ 00261799	Cello	$12.99

Classic Rock

Don't Fear the Reaper • Fortunate Son • Free Fallin' • Go Your Own Way • Jack and Diane • Money • Old Time Rock & Roll • Sweet Home Alabama • 25 or 6 to 4 • and more.

___ 00294356	Flute	$14.99
___ 00294357	Clarinet	$14.99
___ 00294358	Alto Sax	$14.99
___ 00294359	Tenor Sax	$14.99
___ 00294360	Trumpet	$14.99
___ 00294361	Horn	$14.99
___ 00294362	Trombone	$14.99
___ 00294363	Violin	$14.99
___ 00294364	Viola	$14.99
___ 00294365	Cello	$14.99

Contemporary Broadway

Defying Gravity (from Wicked) • Michael in the Bathroom (from Be More Chill) • My Shot (from Hamilton) • Seize the Day (from Newsies) • She Used to Be Mine (from Waitress) • Stupid with Love (from Mean Girls) • Waving Through a Window (from Dear Evan Hansen) • When I Grow Up (from Matilda) • and more.

___ 00298704	Flute	$14.99
___ 00298705	Clarinet	$14.99
___ 00298706	Alto Sax	$14.99
___ 00298707	Tenor Sax	$14.99
___ 00298708	Trumpet	$14.99
___ 00298709	Horn	$14.99
___ 00298710	Trombone	$14.99
___ 00298711	Violin	$14.99
___ 00298712	Viola	$14.99
___ 00298713	Cello	$14.99

Disney Movie Hits

Beauty and the Beast • Belle • Circle of Life • Cruella De Vil • Go the Distance • God Help the Outcasts • Hakuna Matata • If I Didn't Have You • Kiss the Girl • Prince Ali • When She Loved Me • A Whole New World.

___ 00841420	Flute	$12.99
___ 00841421	Clarinet	$12.99
___ 00841422	Alto Sax	$12.99
___ 00841423	Trumpet	$12.99
___ 00841424	French Horn	$12.99
___ 00841425	Trombone/Baritone	$12.99
___ 00841426	Violin	$12.99
___ 00841427	Viola	$12.99
___ 00841428	Cello	$12.99
___ 00841686	Tenor Sax	$12.99
___ 00841687	Oboe	$12.99

Disney Solos

Be Our Guest • Can You Feel the Love Tonight • Colors of the Wind • Friend like Me • Part of Your World • Under the Sea • You'll Be in My Heart • You've Got a Friend in Me • Zero to Hero • and more.

___ 00841404	Flute	$12.99
___ 00841405	Clarinet/Tenor Sax	$12.99
___ 00841406	Alto Sax	$12.99
___ 00841407	Horn	$12.99
___ 00841408	Trombone/Baritone	$12.99
___ 00841409	Trumpet	$12.99
___ 00841410	Violin	$12.99
___ 00841411	Viola	$12.99
___ 00841412	Cello	$12.99
___ 00841506	Oboe	$12.99
___ 00841553	Mallet Percussion	$12.99

Great Classical Themes

Blue Danube Waltz (Strauss) • Can Can (from Orpheus in the Underworld) (Offenbach) • Jesu, Joy of Man's Desiring (J.S. Bach) • Morning Mood (from Peer Gynt) (Grieg) • Ode to Joy (from Symphony No. 9) (Beethoven) • William Tell Overture (Rossini) • and more.

___ 00292727	Flute	$12.99
___ 00292728	Clarinet	$12.99
___ 00292729	Alto Sax	$12.99
___ 00292730	Tenor Sax	$12.99
___ 00292732	Trumpet	$12.99
___ 00292733	Horn	$12.99
___ 00292735	Trombone	$12.99
___ 00292736	Violin	$12.99
___ 00292737	Viola	$12.99
___ 00292738	Cello	$12.99

The Greatest Showman

Come Alive • From Now On • The Greatest Show • A Million Dreams • Never Enough • The Other Side • Rewrite the Stars • This Is Me • Tightrope.

___ 00277389	Flute	$14.99
___ 00277390	Clarinet	$14.99
___ 00277391	Alto Sax	$14.99
___ 00277392	Tenor Sax	$14.99
___ 00277393	Trumpet	$14.99
___ 00277394	Horn	$14.99
___ 00277395	Trombone	$14.99
___ 00277396	Violin	$14.99
___ 00277397	Viola	$14.99
___ 00277398	Cello	$14.99

Irish Favorites

Danny Boy • I Once Loved a Lass • The Little Beggarman • The Minstrel Boy • My Wild Irish Rose • The Wearing of the Green • and dozens more!

___ 00842489	Flute	$12.99
___ 00842490	Clarinet	$12.99
___ 00842491	Alto Sax	$12.99
___ 00842493	Trumpet	$12.99
___ 00842494	Horn	$12.99
___ 00842495	Trombone	$12.99
___ 00842496	Violin	$12.99
___ 00842497	Viola	$12.99
___ 00842498	Cello	$12.99

Simple Songs

All of Me • Evermore • Hallelujah • Happy • I Gotta Feeling • I'm Yours • Lava • Rolling in the Deep • Viva la Vida • You Raise Me Up • and more.

___ 00249081	Flute	$12.99
___ 00249082	Clarinet	$12.99
___ 00249083	Alto Sax	$12.99
___ 00249084	Tenor Sax	$12.99
___ 00249086	Trumpet	$12.99
___ 00249087	Horn	$12.99
___ 00249089	Trombone	$12.99
___ 00249090	Violin	$12.99
___ 00249091	Viola	$12.99
___ 00249092	Cello	$12.99
___ 00249093	Oboe	$12.99
___ 00249094	Keyboard Percussion	$12.99

Stadium Rock

Crazy Train • Don't Stop Believin' • Eye of the Tiger • Havana • Seven Nation Army • Sweet Caroline • We Are the Champions • and more.

___ 00323880	Flute	$14.99
___ 00323881	Clarinet	$14.99
___ 00323882	Alto Sax	$14.99
___ 00323883	Tenor Sax	$14.99
___ 00323884	Trumpet	$14.99
___ 00323885	Horn	$14.99
___ 00323886	Trombone	$14.99
___ 00323887	Violin	$14.99
___ 00323888	Viola	$14.99
___ 00323889	Cello	$14.99

Video Game Music

Angry Birds • Assassin's Creed III • Assassin's Creed Revelations • Battlefield 1942 • Civilization IV (Baba Yetu) • Deltarune (Don't Forget) • Elder Scrolls IV & V • Fallout® 4 • Final Fantasy VII • Full Metal Alchemist (Bratja) (Brothers) • IL-2 Sturmovik: Birds of Prey • Splinter Cell: Conviction • Undertale (Megalovania).

___ 00283877	Flute	$12.99
___ 00283878	Clarinet	$12.99
___ 00283879	Alto Sax	$12.99
___ 00283880	Tenor Sax	$12.99
___ 00283882	Trumpet	$12.99
___ 00283883	Horn	$12.99
___ 00283884	Trombone	$12.99
___ 00283885	Violin	$12.99
___ 00283886	Viola	$12.99
___ 00283887	Cello	$12.99

Prices, contents, and availability subject to change without notice.
Disney characters and Artwork ™ & © 2020 Disney

HAL•LEONARD®